BE A PHANTOM OR A REBEL

ITS YOUR CHOICE

SANJOGITA PAWAR

ISBN 978-93-5458-326-1

Published in India 2021 by Pencil

A brand of
One Point Six Technologies Pvt. Ltd.
123, Building J2, Shram Seva Premises,
Wadala Truck Terminal, Wadala (E)
Mumbai 400037, Maharashtra, INDIA
E connect@thepencilapp.com
W www.thepencilapp.com

Author biography

ABOUT THE AUTHOR.

Sanjogita Pawar is a first year medical student and soon she is going to become a doctor.Her passion for writing developed when she first read "Can't hurt me",by David Goggins.

Through this book the author is trying to contribute some of her experiences for the upcoming generation.

Hope this book can add value to your life.

CONTENTS

$INDEX

1.SELF DOUBT.

1."WE ALL MAKE MISTAKES,HAVE STRUGGLES,AND EVEN REGRET THINGS ARE PAST.BUT YOU ARE NOT YOUR MISTAKES,YOU ARE NOT YOUR STRUGGLES,AND YOU ARE HERE NOW WITH THE POWER TO SHAPE YOUR DAY AND FUTURE."

-

STEVE MARABOLI.

YOU GOT TO BE CAREFULL ABOUT THE THOUGHTS THAT YOU HAVE IN YOUR MIND,SO MANY PEOPLE LIVE THEIR LIFE BY THE LAW OF ACCIDENT,NEVER GRABBING HOLD OFF OF SOMETHING ATTENTIONAL AND DECIDING THAT THESE ARE THE THOUGHTS THAT ARE ALLOWING ME TO LIVE MY LIFE AND ATTENTIONALLY REJECTING OTHER THOUGHTS THAT THEY KNOW ARE GOING GIVE A LIFE THEY ALWAYS WANTED.

2.YOUR "MIND WILL TAKE THE SHAPE OF WHAT YOU FREQUENTLY HOLD IN THOUGHT,FOR THE HUMAN SPIRIT IS COLOURED BY SUCH IMPRESSIONS,

-MARCUS AURELIUS.

AND THATS WHY IT IS SO CRITICAL THAT YOU DECIDE THE THINGS THAT YOUR GOING TO PURSUE MENTALLY,YOU DECIDE WHERE YOUR GOING TO HOLD ON AND YOU HAVE TO MAKE THOSE DECISIONS BASED ON WHAT YOU HAVE DECIDED YOU WANT TO BECOME,BUT IT ALL STARTS FROM KNOWING WAHT IT IS THAT YOU WANNA BECOME,RECOGNIZING THE TRUTH OF THE HUMAN MIND HOW IT WORKS.WHATEVER YOU REPEAT YOU ARE GOING TO BECOME,IF YOU REPEAT SOMETHING EMPOWERING YOU,YOU WILL BECOME EMPOWER,IF YOU REPEAT SOMETHING SELF-DESTRUCTIVE,YOU WILL DESTROY YOURSELF.PEOPLE DONT ACT LIKE ITS TRUE BUT IT IS ACTUALLY TRUE,PEOPLE ACT LIKE THEY ARE SOMETHING IS GOING TO TELL THEM WHO THEY ARE.ONCE THEY HAVE A VISION OF THEMSELVES THAT THEY ARE SIMPLY RECOGNIZING THE TRUTH.BUT THAT 'S THE LIFE,THAT WOULD BE THE GREATEST LIE THAT WE EVER MAKE,THAT WE ARE SOMEHOW STUCK IN TIME,THE ONLY THING IS TO DO IS TO BREAK AND START OVER AGAIN BUT THAT 'S NOT HOW IT WORKS THE WAY ARE HUMAN

BRAIN WORKS.SO,TAKE CONTROL OF THAT PROCESS ,THE SIDE YOU WANNA BECOME NO MATTER HOW DISCOURAGEMENT IT FEELS AT FIRST,YOU GOT TO GO IN PROCESS OF REPETETION IN SHAPING OF YOUR DAY SAME LIKE A SCULPTURE IS GOING THROUGH EVERYDAY AND FINALLY REACHING TO A POINT OF MASTERY.PIECE BY PIECE,BIT BY BIT,DAY AFTER DAY,SO THAT YOU CAN FINALLY REVEAL WHAT YOU WANT TO BECOME.

HERE IS THE HARD TRUTH ABOUT GETTING GREAT,IT TAKES TIME AND DEDICATION,IT TAKES THE WILLINGNESS TO ACCEPT THAT YOU ARE NOT GOOD ENOUGH,ITS THE ABILITY TO STARE PLACES THAT YOU KNOW YOU ARE WEAK AT,AND NOT LETTING IT EFFECT YOUR SELF ESTEEM,NOT LETTING IT EFFECT YOUR CONFIDENCE SO THAT YOU CAN KEEP YOUR MOMEMTUM GOING.YOU HAVE TO UNDERSTAND THAT IN THE BEGINNING WE ALL ARE TERIBLE AND AS "HENRY CARTIER - BRESSON SAID- YOUR FIRST 10,000 PHOTOGRAPHS ARE YOUR WORST".
THE THING THAT MAKES PEOPLE TO BE GREAT ARE PEOPLE WHO CONTINUESLY PUSH THEMSELVES.GREATNESS IS A HABIT THAT YOU FOLLOW EVERYDAY,BIT BY BIT,ITS BEING UNAFRAID TO MAKE THOSE MISTAKES,ITS BEING TO ACCEPT THAT YOU ARE NOT YET GREAT.

3.MARY ANNE RADMACHER ONCE SAID,COURAGE DOESN'T ALWAYS ROAR,SOMETIMES COURAGE IS THE QUIET VOICE AT THE END OF THE DAYSAYING,Í WILL TRY AGAIN TOMORROW'.IF YOU WANNA BE GREAT THAT WHAT YOU HAVE TO DO,GET UP AGAIN TOMORROW,YOU GOT TO BE WILLING TO FACE TOMORROW,YOU GOT TO BE ACCEPT THAT THE ROAD TOO FAR TO REST,YOU SHOULD BE LOOKING FOR PEOPLE WHO ALWAYS TEACH YOU SOMETHING,ALWAYS TRY TO LEARN FROM EACH AND EVERY PERSON YOU MEET,LEARN FROM EACH EVERY EXPERIENCE THAT YOU HAVE GONE THROUGH.PEOPLE WHO YOU ARE LOOKING UPTO TODAY,THEY ARE ONCE THAT LISTEN TODAY,THE ONCE THAT SPENT THEIR EVERY OUNCE OF THEIR DAY TODAY ,USE THEIR ENERGY TODAY,MASTERING,GETTING BETTER EVERYDAY,RELENTLESSLY LOOKING AT THING AND TRYING TO IMPROVE DAY BY DAY,THOSE ARE PEOPLE WE REMEMBER,SO IF YOU WANNA BE REMEMBERED,IF YOU WANNA ACHEIVE REAL GREATNESS,YOU JUST NEED TO HAVE THE COURAGE TO SHOW UP EVERYDAY, TRY ANOTHER TASK, DO SOMETHING THAT SCARES YOU.

DO THOSE LITTLE THINGS OVER AND OVER UNTIL YOU WIN.AS OPRAH WINFREY SAID,"WHAT YOU DWELL ON IS WHAT YOU

BECOME".
ONCE YOU UNDERSTAND THAT THE HUMANS ARE THE ADAPTATION MACHINE,AND YOU UNDERSTAND THAT THE BRAIN BUILDS FASTER AND BETTER CONNECTION BETWEEN THE THINGS THAT YOU BEGIN TO UNDERSTAND,ITS INCREDIBLE TO UNDERSTAND WHAT YOU WANT TO BECOME WITHOUT UNDERESTIMATING YOUR OWN POTENTIALS.

If you dont think that you are not good enough,change the way you practice,give another shot,if you are not happy with your results,you need to put in efforts,ypu need to sacrifice for your dream to come true.If you want to make an impact on this world,first you have to make an impact on yourself.
Its the suffering that will make you great,its a suffering that will make you tough,its a suffering that will make you keep going,because in that suffering,you can becarne anything you want,become a vision of what you always wanted,and you are going to become.

As Will Smith said,"the separation of talent and skill is one of the most misunderstood concepts for people who are trying to excel,who have dreams,who want to do things.Talent you have naturally,Skill is only developed by hours and hours,of beating on your carft".

That 's what I want everybody to understand those who feel useless,feel like they 're not good as other people,they feel like they have no worth and no value,they dont believe in themselves is because they are not understanding the difference between talent and skill.Dont worry about that,not everybody has great talent,but the person who has workethic is the person who will definetely do something great in his/her life,you need to focus on your daily day to day actions,you need to fullfill your empty life with purposeful dream,you need to have a discipline life if you want to achieve things in life.The fruit of everything great begins with a challenge,you need to develop your workethic,your schedule,your way of looking upto your life.

The moment you decide to take control of your life, the half battle is automatically won.

There was once a guy who was always fascinated to join the defense forces, he was so passionate about being in the Indian Uniform that he gave the exams, he got selected in the armed forces, done his graduating parade and when he was getting commissioned as an officer the next day he met with an accident and the left side of his body got paralyzed, from then life for him was tough to tackle. He wanted to end his life, because he thought that his only dream was to join the Indian defense Forces and serve his country but this accident had turned his life upside down, he started having suicidal tendencies and he decided that he is going to live for 7 days and on the 8 day he is going to end his life. He decided that the 1 and 2nd day will be for his friend, 3 and 4 th day will be for animals and last 3 days he will spent his day with his family, he lived his life for this 7 days and on the 8th day he went to bedroom, just was going to finish his life by cutting his nerves on his wrist and a glance of his memories appeared in front of him, the moment he kept the knife on his wrist he stopped and thought that he belonged to a defense background he cannot end his life just with a knife, what is a big deal that his left side of his body is paralyzed he can still do things in his life and he needs to find out ways to do it, he was talking to himself for sometime and figuring ways out ,what next, and the first thing that got up to his mind was that he was a great speaker, he thought that why not he can be a motivational speaker, and the answers he got himself from within and now he is worlds number one motivational speaker that world has ever know.

Over here we are trying to let you know that the lowest moments of your life are going to make you the best version of yourself, just believe in yourself and believe in your instinct, the right thing will come automatically to you, you just need to self analyze things.

2.HOW THE BRAIN WORKS.

How The Brain Works....

We all have some behaviour that we would like to change about ourselves and we certainly all want to help someone else change their behaviour in a positive way,so maybe it is your kid,your colleague….

I want to share some new research with you that I think reveals something very important about what gets people to change their behaviour.But before I do that lets zoom into one strategy that I think you probably use a lot.

Lets take an easy example – ypu are trying to stop yourself from snacking .What do you say to yourself??- well most people,in a monologue will say "Beware you'll be fat".And if this was your younger sibling,you would probably tell him that smoking kills and by the way,his is a big trouble…..So,what were trying to do here is we're trying to scare ourselves and others into changing their behaviour,and it is not just us.Warnings and threats are really common in health campaignsin policy.

Its because we all share this deep rooted belief that if you threaten people,if fear is induced it will get them to act.It seema like a really reasonable assumption,except for the fact that the science shows that "WARNINGS HAVE A VERY LIMITED IMPACT ON ARE BEHAVIOUR".So, graphic images on cigarette packets for example;do not deter smokers from smoking and one study foung that after looking at those images,quiting actually became a lower priority for smokers.

Here we are not saying that warnings and threats never work,but what we are trying to explain how the brain works,the warnings seem to have a very limited impact and so the question is why??Why are we resistant to warnings??

Well,if you think about animals,when you induce fear in a animal,the mostcommon response you will see is freezing or fleein;fighting not as much and so humans are the same.So,if something scares us we tend to shut down and we try to eliminate the negative feelings.

So,we might use rationalization…..for example- "my grandpa smoked,He lived to be 90.So,I have a better genes and absolutely nothing to worry about it.

And this process can actually make you feel more resilient than you did before

Which is why warnings sometimes we have this boomerang effect.In others times we simply put are head in the ground.Take the stock market for example- Do you know when people pull their head out of the ground to look at their account not to make any transactions,just to log in to check their account and the following data and assumption is made by KARLESSON LOWENSTEIN and SEPPI.When the market is high people log in all the time,because positive information makes you feel good,so you seek it out and when the market is low,people avoid logging in because negative information makes us feel bad, so we try to avoid it altogether and all this is true as long as bad information can reasonablybe avoided.So,what do you need to know is 14 years back in the financial collapse of 2008,when the market went drastically down and that was when people started logging in frantically,but it was too late.You can think about it like this-its not just finance.

In many different parts of are life as time passes you gather more and more information about where the wing is blowing and at any point,you can intervene and you could potentially change the outcome,but that takes energy and you might tell yourself.'What s' the point about worrying about something that might happen or might not happen.Until we reach this point at which time you do jump into action,but sometimes it's a little bit too late.

An experiment was conducted by experts in America,where they asked appropriately 100 people to estimate the likelyhood of 80 different negative events that might happen to them in the future.For example- they might ask you,"whats the likelyhood that you'll suffer hearing loss in the future??

And lets say you think its about 50%Then I give you the opinion of 2 different experts.So, Expert A tells you – for someone like you,I think the hearing loss in your future will be 40%. So, they give you a rosier view of your future.

Expert B says- for someone like you I actually think that its about 60%,its worse.They give you a bleaker view of your future.What should you??Well,you should n't change your beliefs right?WRONG.

What they found was is that people tend to change their beliefs towards a more desirable opinion.In other words,people listen to the positive information.Now,this study was conducted on college students,so you might say,well college student are delusional right?We all know that?And surely as we grow older,we grow wiser.So,the experts said lets test that does this really generalize?Does this generalize to your parent?Your kid?You younger cousins?

They tested people from the age of 10 until the age of 80,and the answer was yes.In all these age groups,people take in information they want to hear like someone telling you you're more intelligent than your thought than information that they don't want to hear And the ability to learn from goodnews,it remained quite stable throughout the lifespan.But the ability to learn from bad news,that changes as you age.So,what we found was that kids and teenagers-they were the worse at learning from bad news and the ability became better and better as people aged.

But then, around the age of 40 around midlife it started deteriorating again.What this means is that the most vulnerable population kids and teenagers on one hand,and the other hand,they are the least likely to accurately learn from warnings.But what you can see hear is that it doesn't matter what age you are,you can be 20,30,40,50,etc everyone takes information they want to hear more than information that they don't.

Our mistakes as elders,teachers,and as mentors is that instead of working with this positive image that people so effortfully maintain in their brain?We try and put a clear mirror in front of them.We tell them "YOU KNOW,THE IMAGE IS GOING TO GET WORSE AND WORSE",and it doesn't work.It doesn't work because the brain will frantically try to distort the image using photoshop and fancy lenses until it gets the image he/she is happy with.

But what would happen if we went along with how are brain works and not against it?

Take handwashing for example:-

We all know that handwashing is the number one way to prevent the spread of diseases and this is really important in hospitals.

In a hospital in the united states,a camera was installed to see how often medical staff do infact sanitize their hands before and after entering a patients room.

Now,the medical staff knew a camera was installed.Nevertheless,only one in ten washed their hands before and after entering a patients rooms.But then an intervention was introduced, a electronic board that told the medical staff how well they were doing.Everytime they washed their hands the numbers went up the screen and it showed their rate of their current shift and the rate of the weekly staff.And what happened?BOOOM compliance raised to 90%,which is absolutely amazing and the research staff were amazed as well and they made sure to replicate it in another division in the hospital, again the same results were updated.

So, why does this intervention works so well?? It works well because instead of using warnings about bad things that can happen in the future,like diseases,it uses 3 principles:- that we really drive your mind and your behaviour.

The first one is the:1.Social Incentives;

In the hospital study the medical staff could see what other people were doing,they can see the rates of the shift,the rate of the week.

We are social people,we really care what other people are doing.,we want to do the same,and we want to do it better.The British government uses this techniques to get people to pay their taxes on the time.

In old letter,that they sent to people who forgot to pay their taxes on time,they added one sentence and sentence said,"NINE OUT OF TEN PEOPLE IN BRITAIN PAY THEIR TAXES ON TIME",and that one sentence enhanced compliance within that group by 15% and its thought to bring into the british government 5.6 billion pounds.

So,highlighting what other people are doing is a really strong incentive.

The second principal=3.IMMEDIATE REWARD.

Everytime the staff wash their hands they could see the numbers go up on the board and it made them feel good,knowing that in advance made them do something that they otherwise may not want to do.

Now,this grows because we value immediate rewards that we can get now more than rewards that we can get in the future.What will happen if you reward people now for doing actions that are good for them in the future.

Studies show that giving people immediate rewards makes them more likely to quit smoking and start exercising,this effect lasts upto six months because not smoking becomes associated with a reward and it becomes a habit,it becomes a lifestyle.

The third principal=3.PROGRESS MONITORING.

So, the electronic board focused the medical staff attention on improving their performance.Brain does a really good job,but it doesn't do such a good job at processing negative information about the future.So,what does this means,it means that if you're trying to get people s attention,you might want to highlight the progress not the decline.For example;If you take that kid with the cigarette,you might want to tell them: "You know,if you stop smoking you'll become better at sports.

HIGHLIGHT THE PROGRESS NOT THE DECLINE.

Even in your life,when you are judging yourself, judge yourself with good things and decline the negative things it will help you to improve and have a sense of proud feeling foryourself which is very important to start on the process of success.

3.STARTING THE PROCESS.

HOW TO START THE PROCESS…

To start the process for getting into the journey of success….to get started first you need to change your mentality and start highlighting the progress and not the decline just we learned how to do it in the previous chapter.

Let`s begin: Find the person who is living your ideal/dream life.Go to them and say the following,'I will work for you for free for the next 90 days.I will work harder and smarter than anyone you have ever met'.

And when you get in,over deliver.

You better shock them,you better leave them in appreciation mind.

Nothing is below you,you are willing to do everthing.

You hustle harder then anybody,and you are doing it all for no money,and lastly you say to them.

"If at the end of these 90 days,you would rather pay me than loose me 'GREAT' I have a job.If not we shake hands and part ways.All I ask in return is knowledge and connection".

Those two things will monetize forever.The mistake everybody makes when they get out of school is they try to get as much money as humanly possible.Money can only be spent once but knowledge monetizes forever.

Just remember that money can be easily made and infact we can earn money in any and every field it is just the matter of time,work,action,and choices.Knowledge is something which cannot be purchased but earned through continue efforts,research,communication,reading,listening to knowledgeable minds etc.

Just give yourself time,understand yourself,explore things and see what is fascinating to you,what is that one thing you cannot live without,you cant imagine your life without that thing and once you find that thing start studying about it,try to get knowledge as much as possible through online materials,try to communicate with people who are already in that field and lastly start taking necessary actions to get into the game.

4.CHOICES MAKES THE MOVE GOING.

CHOICES MAKES THE MOVE GOING…

Everyone experiences things differently.Two people can go through the same experiences and feel two different ways about it.

We all have a choice but how we perceive our life,forms the choices we think we have.

Recognize that we all have a choice to make a decision to improve are life no matter how hard times are hitting on you right now, you have a choice to either be in the same situation and do nothing about it or deal with your problem and fixit and make a difference in your life for a better future.

Wayne Dyer once said that "When you look at the things,the things you look at change".We can either repeat others mistakes or relearn how to live.

Its our choice.We can either copy bad behaviour or learn to cope with good behaviour.It is are choice.We can either make the same mistake or take the opportunity to find the solution.

ITS YOUR CHOICE.

5. THE IKA EXPERT.

THE IKA EXPERT…..

Lets understand about what is an IKA EXPERT with an example,

You wake up,before you even grab your cell phone.You say,"Today is the day that I m going to be proactive.

Im going to take control of my life.Im going to see a doctor,I m going to get healthy.

So,you sacrifice your dayoff work,You sit in one hour standstill traffic,you even wait for 30 minutes in the office to a see a doctor.Finally the walks in and all of that built up anxiety begins to fade.

In the middle of your converstion you ask the doctor a few questions,"Doctor what`s the healthiest diet"? You get back an answer "I DON'T KNOW".

You say okay,"Doctor I have a respiratory virus,which virus is it"? Again you get an answer 'I DON'T KNOW'.

Your mind begins to wonder whether or not this doctor was properly educated.

Finally you ask,"Doctor what is the reason that the rate of autism is increasing". And the answer is again 'I DON'T KNOW'.Your frustration hits peak…..

Lets stop this hypothetical for a second.There is a reason why you shoud`nt be frustrated and instead celebrate those who are not afraid to say 'I DON'T KNOW'.

We are going to acclaim all the 'IKA EXPERT' or the 'I KNOW ALL EXPERTS'.The IKA experts claims to have all the answers when the rest of the scientific community has questions.

Now this may surprise you but you and I are both partially responsible if not more so,blame for this epidemic.

When someone says to us they don't know,we`re quick to judge,we`re are quick to dismiss.

We click on the catchy headlines within medicine,there are two specific situations where these IKA experts flourish.

The first is the grey zone,that is when a question within the field of medicine or any research field has not yet had an complete answer by modern science.

'Take the increase rate of autism,you ask an honest person about this they'll say I DON'T KNOW,but if ask this same question to an IKA expert they will throw you a theory and they'll do it in a very convincing fashion.

So much so that they might even further their career in one way or another.Thats the problem with this IKA experts.

The second way that they do this is they do it in moments where good medicine has proved that tangible positive effect is only achieved through hardwork and dedication.

Take diet,take exercise,take sleep,etc the way to improve all of these is through harwork.

But the IKA expert will give a shortcut and I am sure many of you have heard of these shortcuts.

Take for instances the shortcut of the miracle weight loss diet known as the cookie diet or better yet the miracle detox plan.How do these IKA expert cause you to ignore the legitimate scientific evidence, advice and listen to your theories?They do so through stress.

When your mind is stressed,your mind is very easily influenced.Your mind does not respond to well to stress as a survical mechanism,your mind uses stress as a way to be influenced by the majority.

So,what these IKA expert do is they throw around words like cancer,disease,fear,anxiety,adrenaline,death,even your family involved at times and that's how they got you.

A marketer s job is to sell products or to push a brand and they do so by studying the human psyche to figure out the best way to accomplish their profits.

We live in a fast paced world.We want quick answers and even faster results,but before you go on this desperate search for answers and shortcuts, lets see about what a true expert is;A true expert not only looks at the current most updated scientific evidence,but also looks at the history as a guide.

How many times have you heard doctors go back and forth on the health benefits of risks of coffee,something we all drink everyday?

In 1981,the New York Times published a study thst said 2 cups of coffee increases the risk of pancreatic cancer.In 2017,we claimed that coffee extends your life rate.

Doctors used to advocate smoking as a stress reliever.

We used to believe that bloodletting-AKA-letting a patient bleedout,was a way to cure an infection.

This doesn't mean that doctors are not smart what this actually means is that expert opinion is and should be considered the lowest form of evidence.That is what are job as a true expert – is to explain that to the general population.

Take any PHD person around the you and they'll all tell you the samething,the more years they have spent studying a subject,the more they realize they don't know,the more questions you have,more you realize you don't know.

More questions you have good,it's a sign of intelligence.

Now,look this isn't just a theoretical discussion where we're going to see about philosophical change and things of that nature but going to see some practical tips on what you should actually do.

NUMBER1; ASK BETTER QUESTIONS.

For example,if a doctor prescribes a treatment or tells you not to go for a treatment,ask him/her,'Hey doctor why do I need these antibiotics. When an IKA expert claims there is a miserable cure for whatever ails you,ask how is it possible that there are million of doctors across the world whose sole and only mission is to eradicate diseases and restore optimal health don't agree with them.

Why is it the same 5 IKA expert you see appearing in documentaries talking about doom and gloom from all the things that ail you.

NUMBER2; UNDERSTAND BASIC RESEARCH.

Often times these IKA expert will doubt a single study and try to convince you of their theories.Take the recent uproar of autism and childhood immunization.

This uproar started from a single study with 12 subjects which was done by a doctor.

Whoes been discredited and lost their license and yet children are dying.So, its your job to be aware of this research and here 's how to do it,known that best form of research is a metanalysis.Its a combination of studies,not just one which allows for the decreased likelihood of chance and bias within their results.

Note that newer studies are not necessarily better than older one.

Known that studies that focuses on diseases markers are not nearly as good as studies that focus on outcomes and development of diseases.And no matter what media tells,or any other unknowlegable person tells you are a breakthrough,there is no single study that will influence the field of medicine or any other field or industry enough to change the standard of case it can guide us.

It can put itself into the context of the entire body of evidence to allow us to figure out what the true result are and what they mean.

NUMBER3;DO NOT WRITE OFF OR BLAME ANY PERSON WHO SAYS THEY DON'T KNOW;

Instead of judging people on the basis of their answers just know about their experiences,their mistakes,their story.It will help you the most to build your courier.Take for example-a doctor,don't judge him/her on their first instance if they are telling they don't know,but celebrate that this doctor is selfaware and most importantly he/she is not interested in slimming your wallet.

The greatest experience you will always get in your failures or hardtimes.The hardtimes will decide your personality,your limitations.Just grind and shine and just remember that "TOUGH TIMES DO NOT LAST BUT TOUGH PEOPLE DO".

6. SETTING GOALS.

SET GOALS AND ACHIEVE THEM.

Setting goals is very important as it is the very most basic rule of life….today I am gonna share some of my secrets,..

Step1::Be specific not vague,what do I mean by that is you need to set your goals specifically and vague for example-if you want to grow your business you must be having an idea to grow your business until this year but my suggestion is if you want to achieve that success by the end of the year you need to think that what action you should take today to achieve that goal in the future.Break your goals into monthly,weekly and daily basis goal only then you can achieve and see your results by the end of the year,I call this method as REVERSE ENGINE.

Step 2::Set goals in major areas of your life,now there are 4 major areas 1-Health,if you don't have a good health no matter how successful you are it's all waste.2-Relation,you have to give time to your parents, friends,kids and even the hobby that you enjoy in short live your life according to your choices.3-Finance,you need to invest your time in this area very specifically as this is the area which will generate your income.4-contribution, whatever you have accieved or you have, need to share it with people and contribute.But according to me as we all are humans we cannot balance all this areas in one go so my suggestion to you is decide from which areas it will be easy to achieve goals and by which area you can even balance your other areas as well,if you ask I would prefer to give my 80% to the financial area because automatically If I manage to get my finance strong I can contribute it,my health issues will be perfect,I can spend my time with my family.The decision is upto to you in which area you are right now.

Step3::Achieve your goal automagically,Yes thats right AUTOMAGICALLY:by this I mean to say that to achieve your goal you need to first set your goal,write it on a piece of paper, 2_See it everyday , see your goal everyday by setting-writting-and pasting in front of your study table,office table.Remember, wherever energy goes, attention goes,energy flows, result s shows.3_ Live it , you have to live your goal to achieve it this was said by Albert Einstein when he was busy doing one of his experiment in America,you have to live like you have already been there.If you want to buy a Ferrari ,you need to drive a Ferrari doesn't mean you need to buy but a test drive can be usefull,to achieve it you need to live it and even experience.You have to see yourself live that life before you have that life.4_The next one is Share it,the goals which you are having try to share it with people you know,now there can be one question fromyour side as what if I cannot achieve my goal,what will others think of me if I share my goal with them---you see if you don't have confidence on your self I guarantee you that you won't succeed ,it's all about the mindset you have to achieve your goal you need to share it aswell and challenge yourself.

I am gonna leave you with one thought :::::Live your life as if all your dreams have come true and then challenge your reality to catch up…….Till then keep hustling.

7. WHEN TO QUIT.

WHEN TO QUIT……..

Winners don't quit and quitters don't win.

But how do you know when to quit and when to continue… You have always heard of the beleif , well sometimes in business you gotta zig and zag you gotta pivot ,that is the word.Somethings doesn't work,you try something else but how do you know if your actually pivotting or it's just like a shiny object syndrome for you?What is right?How do you know when to quit…. How many times you have tried something in your business and you have been doing that business for sometime now,maybe for years ,and it's going a little bit ,but it's going anywhere soon and you ask yourself should I Quit?You should know when you quote on quote ,quit?I failed in some part of my life but learnt stuffs from every failure that I faced before having my first success.So if you have challenges knowing when to quit,You require to do some very deep thinking.So,how do you know when to quit.

The answer is Self Awareness,what is self awareness- It is the capacity to stand apart from yourself , and examine your actions ,your history,your motive,your drive,your habits.Self awareness involve deep personal honesty.It requires you to ask a very tough and hard questions like:1:Should I invest in real estate,:2:tell me something about cryptocurrency ,:3:I am in this situation what should I do ?-----All these questions sell low self awareness.Low self awareness period ,you don't understand yourself,the awareness is so low,that you are not even sure what you should do ,it's not even a clarity issue-its an self awareness issue.For example--Lets say someone says I started a business,should I continue or quit ,should I give up , what should I do with this business, instead of just asking someone about it,you should ask yourself first.

How would you ask it or see it.Question arises self awareness in action,the question you should ask or ask yourself is 1:::Why are you even in this business in the first place?What motivates you to start this business?Does this business fit your natural talents and strengths?And what qualifies you to be in this business.2:::What's your edge?What's your plan for growth ? Now you have been doing this for sometime,you are making any progress ?Or are you just

getting further in debt ?Do you have a plan to grow in the next 3,4,5 years ?Let's say you have the right people and team to help you to take your business to next level ?And if the business is losing money ,how much cash in the bank is there that you could still use before you go bankrupt? And if you are not producing the results you are looking for what skills set that you need to develop , in order to produce results ,maybe it's copywritting,selling, marketing,closing, communication,generating traffic to your website etc,I don't know you but you should know you ,all these questions,if you can answer those,you'll have a very clear idea if you should quit or not and that's why people look to a third party because they don't have patience,look to me to look to somebody else and tell them you should quit or when to quit . It's not an simple answer.Its all self awareness and that's why I like what Bruce Lee said "All knowledge ultimately leads to self knowledge".Knowing one's self,knowing yourself ,but unfortunately the sad part is many young entrepreneurs fail because of low self awareness,their attention span is so short and that's why they don't succeed but suffer so be aware of yourself. ARE YOU AMONG THEM WHO THINKS OR SHARES???????

8.PROCASTION THE EVIL.

Procastination equals poverty.

##There are only three ways to deal with this procastination syndrome.Tony Robbins once said that procastination equals poverty.

I am gonna discuss 3rules that you should follow to overcome this syndrome,Number-1Work hard,people always say that working hard is not my type and I'll do smart work but let me tell you that people who follow this one never succeed because they don't have any sort of work ethic,now that's right WORKETHIC you may consider this as a irrelevant quotient but this is the

rule of the game of life,you need to learn workethich first to acheive your goals,now to gain WORKETHIC you need to learn workhard ,no matter what your age is you might be a student who never wants to study,may be a business man with a small startup ,here what I suggest is that take that extra class that you never wanted to take,take action against your business and try to fix it as the company only reflects it's founders mindset,take that extra lap in every aspect of your life no matter how hard you tried in short- come out of your comfort zone and take ACTION.

Number 2- Smartwork,Now you have learnt the basics, you know what is workethich , try to work smart,think where you are lacking and take vice decision, you should know where you should invest your time and money and where you shouldn't.As Martin Luther King once said time is the most precious thing and the only thing which cannot come back Take decisions vicely.

Number3-Think Smart,Henry Ford once said that the most difficult thing is to think and because of which most people fail to reach there goals.You need to think smart because all questions and doubts which you are having can be cured and solved by yourselves but people don't want to think and this is where they lack.So, out of 99 people only 2-3% will follow this rules and achieve what they want in there life.DO YOU COME IN THIS 2-3% CATAGORIE?????.

9.THE FINAL CHAPTER

THE FINAL CHAPTER:WHEN IT HURTS…..

I wanna encourage you if you are thinking about quitting and giving up.If you are praying for years for things to turn around.You're thinking about quitting,you are folding,you are caving in.This is for you.You're in this storm and you're down on your knees,you're cold,you're weak and you feel like this is the end.You have a choice to either give up or keep going.

"GIVE UP OR GET UP".DONT GIVE UP.STAY IN IT.

Stay focussed.If you fail,try again,and again.You just take one step at a time.Its hard but its worth fighting.Its worth believing.Its worth mustering yourself up,standing up inside yourself.Its worth fighting relentlessly.Never giving up.We love the sun but things don't grow because of the sun,you have to have some rain and you have stop looking at rain in your life as something bad.My greatest moments didn't come from my greatest moments because it was during my defeat that I had to find a way to get back up.Just imagine this for yourself;you thought for a minute that your haters thought that they broke you,they got you twisted,they made you feel phenomenally not skilled but unfortunately they got you phenomenally willed.You will not surrender,you will not quit.DON'T STOP.Don't stop runningtowards your dreams.Stay encouraged.Keep your head up.Continue to walk with pride,and know,if it was easy everybody would do it.Its not gonna be easy,but we have what it takes.The rough times are gonna come but they have not come here to stay,they have come to pass.Don't say you are having a bad day,say I am having a character building day.Don't look at night as darkness,look at night as a new beginning….

To be successful,you need to love the process,the ultimate goal of yours will be automatically achieved.If you are in your teens,you will be facing difficulties for the first time,there will be sleepless night,self doubts,hardships but you got to know that everthing will be alright.Just focus on yourself,do your work,and find what is the true meaning of life for you.

Now there is a common question that everybody asks is how do you find your passion….the simple answer to the simple question is explore as many of things you can,throw yourself into each and every activity you have in your school,college,university,or any other online platform.Get yourself as much experience as you can in every field that you think exists and lastly know your worth,your time is precious don't spend it on people who are not important to you.World 's most expensive gift is your TIME,safe it if you wanna make it big.

What 's stopping you?Are you too tired?Didn't get enough sleep?Dont have enough energy?Dont have enough time?Is that stopping you right now?Dont have enough money?Is that the thing?Or is the thing thats stopping you?YOU?Excuses sound the best to the person who 's making them up.Stop feeling sorry foryourself,telling everybody you're sad,if you feel jealous of people who get down from a Rolls royce,or living in a 6 or 7 starhotel,dont get jealous of them because they have worked like hell to get that sort of lifestyle.Nobody handed them nothing,instead awaken the beast inside.Its game on,its go season,its time for you to take the advantage of the resources that you have today in your country and your community.You got a problem with your life? You got a problem with your envioursment?Do something about it.If you want it,go get it.

Recognise that the execuses are not valid.They are conjured up,they are fabricated,they are lies.

How do you stop the lies,you stop the lies by telling the truth.And the truth is you have time,you have the skill,you have the knowledge,you have the support,the will power,and the discipline to get it done.The fruit of everything good in life begins with a challenge.Everything is uphill that's worthwhile,and its not going to come to you,its not going to fall in your lap,its not going to be something "Oh my ghosh",it was just so simple,it is always going to be difficult.If you want it bad enough you have to work hard enough.This is your chance,this is your moment,this is your time,this is your place,this is your opportunity to prove your haters wrong,there is no such thing called tomorrow, we only got today.Stay on the basketball ground,stay on the football field,take that extra maths class,take that extra mile.Its gring season champ.

ITS WORTH DOING.

10. LESSON TO REMEMBER.

THE ONLY LESSON...

The lesson that I learnt while growing up was that every activity that I wanted to perform or complete would take only few changes in mindset.There is a research done by scientists that it takes 5 seconds for your brain to take action upon things which you are thinking of doing,its a very basic and simple process but a very powerful one.

Most people fail just because either they have lost interest in doing what they do or they are not able to make up their mind.The very basic thing is that if you set a goal and just start making roadmaps on how to reach towards your goals,half of the battle is already won,but unfortunately most people fail in the very first step.To become successful,rich etc you need to first have a plan,then you just start the process,start taking actions on it,set daily routine goals or short term goals as these mini goals will help you to reach your long term goals.Focus on yourself,dont bother what others are telling you to do,if you are pretty sure that you cannot imagine your life without some specific things you are on the right track,to be a master in any field you just need 1,000 hours which is 2 to 3 years.Master in any skill you like and be consistent with it,there is no one who could defeat you,but first

concentrate on your own stuff.
There will be problems when you first make your decisions but dont get disheartened,time will come when people will understand that you were right.
Don't depend on people to approve your work and just remember that even are own shadows leave us in the dark.
STAY FOCUSSED,STAY HUNGRY,
The last word to remember;"TOUGH TIMES DO NOT LAST, BUT TOUGH PEOPLE DO".

11. STOP WASTING TIME.

Somebody said,"Downtime was the time you spend doing things that prevent you from moving up in life".Tell me how are you using your free time and I will tell you your future.How are you spending your downtime,are you killing time or you are giving life to it.How are you spending your recreation or "RE-CREATION",so many people are recreating themselves into a version of themselves.Your downtime has to be spent on doing things to move you up,to become the most highest well developed version of yourself.When you are in your car,turnoff the radio,turnoff the music,most people who makes money make money off of filling our heads with ideas that they dont even let thier children listen to because by copying someone will never make you successful.When you listen to music what you do?You nod your head,sending a message to your body 's subconcious message saying YES,I agree with what i am listening to on the radio.I agree with it.So,if you are not careful,you could be subconciously agreeing with a message that is not in the best interest of your highest self.People say,You are what you eat,that is true,but you are also what you see,you are what you ear,you are what you do all day,so if you don't program your mind,your mind will be programmed for you by the radio programmer.

They call it back to your regular scheduled

programming.So, if it doesn't give you highest benefit of your time or the best version of yourself,don't listen to it.Don't watch it.Don't touch it.Don't do it.You pay a note everymonth for your car,your car needs to be paying back in the form of knowledge.Instead of the radio,listen to podcast,audiobooks,on subjects that are in harmony with the life that you want to create.Turn your car into an automobile degree,if you listen to a chapter everyday within two to three years you can be in the top 5% of your industry.You pay a bill everymonth for your cellphone,your mobile needs to be paying you back in the form of value,knowledge.Spending time on your instagram and waisting time instead follow pages that are in harmony with your highest,best and most developedversion of yourself.I can promise you that if you spend your downtime into timewell spent,then you can eventually have your passtime turn into fulltime in no time.

12. BRAIN THEORY.

BRAIN THEORY......
I just went for a walk in a park and I saw that two boys were teasing a girl because she was wearing her #filas shoes,now as that girl was not a material person she replied that why she was wearing her filas on and here it goes- "You two boys nice to meet you and for your kind information I just wore my filas shoes just because I like the color,I think they are cool,they might not be as popular today but you know that's what I like.Its not about what I have on feet,it's about what I have in my head-No matter what I am wearing,no matter what I have on,it's about the information,the knowledge in my life.These sneakers are not even going to fit you in 20 years from now,so what you have in your mind is your wisdom,your knowledge,your power to inspire others"..... WOWWWWWWWWWWW!!!! WE NEED KIDS LIKE THISSSSS. This sought of mindset can only be seeded in are generation and coming generations if we guide them.... especially (parents)- Please don't raise your children like the materialistic type..because once they don't have Jordans on or cool clothes they gonna feel like they are not important,they gonna feel like they need golden,Jordans,cool stuff on,"popular stuff" on to make themselves feel important. Give your children such foundation that they can make their own empire...

13. IRONMAN THEORY.

IRONMAN THEORIES....

I have always been fascinated about superheroes growing up,but Ironman is a character which does not have any superpowers but is a superhero??Why??Because "Tony Stark"- (THE IRONMAN),is smart,he has brain,he knows what he is good at. IRONMAN RULE #1: BE YOUR BIGGEST FAN = In this video,you'll see Tony's always very sure of himself,even when Captain America is challenging him,He knows he doesn't have superpowers or super strength,but he knows what he is good at =Same in are life we don't do what we known we 're supposed to do,because of lack of confidence and self-esteem,we don't believe,we don't know if it's gonna work or it's not gonna work,what if it fails???? That lack of self esteem,that lack certainty. "BUT SELF-ESTEEM IS THE FOUNDATION OF ALL SUCCESS". Just imagine if you just do what you know,your supposed to do,if you truly believe in yourself,and "BE YOUR OWN BIGGEST FAN".How much further you'll be in life???How much more successful you will be??????

14.IRONMAN THEORY 2.

IRONMAN THEORIES...2..

IRONMAN RULE ##2 "CONFIDENCE COMES FROM COMPETENCE". One of the reasons why Tony is so confident about himself is because he's got the mindset,he's got the skillsets,he knows what he is capable of,Not because of fancy equipment or an lavish lab,or anything like that,just like what you saw in the clip,he built his suit in the cave,because of his ability,because of his mind. So,very often,if you want to be more confident or in certain areas,if you lack confidence,ask yourself,how much time have spent on developing the skillset?????Honing your craft getting good at.When you are good at something naturally,you"ll be more confident.So,ask yourself in certain areas of life,which area that you need work on. In Which area you want to develop more confidence. When you are more confident, you'll be more #Determined as well. The choice is yours. #young#boss#mindset#work#leadership#success#inspiration

15.IRONMAN THEORY 3.

IRONMAN THEORIES...

IRONMAN RULE###3. COMMUNICATE CONFIDENTLY..... I truly believe what holds people back,is lack of confidence but most of the time it is lack of communication skill.You,see Tony Stark is an phenomenal communicator,very charismatic,very confident,not only he feels confidence,but he knows how to communicate.... This strategy can be used in are daily lifestyle as well to be successful in life as now because of social media,we all are working from the computer, laptop,the phone, that even young people ,they don't know how to talk to people anymore????We don't know how to communicatc,bccausc all the communication we do is from text RIGHT????But how do you express yourself confidently,one on one,on the phone or to a camera??? So,that it will have more impact in your courier,life,your income,way more than you think,it is through practice.If you want to improve your communication skills you have to practice in real life not by any video content,not by listening to any podcast,but just by standing in front of the mirror and talking to yourself with any random topic you have your interest in and then practising the same thing with your friends,family,teachers etc. So,if you want to be more successful in life you have to improve your communication skills and to improve you have to practice.

16.IRONMAN THEORY 4.

IRONMAN THEORIES...

IRONMAN RULE ####4 #MAKE SACRIFICES FOR THE THING YOU LOVE. Very often,we see people that say I want this,I want to do this,I will have these goals and I want to be more successful but they are not willing to sacrifice.There s always a pay price to action,if you want something,you have to give something.What are you willing to give?What are you willing to sacrifice to get what you want? If you wanna make $40,000 a year spend time with family,have that work life balance,that's perfectly fine,that's goodlife."BUT" if you wanna make six figure,a million dollars a year,let us face the truth there's no suchthing as work life balance.You have to be willing to sacrifice.I am not saying you have to be #workaholic ,what am I saying is in order to build your career,to build your business to take it to next level,there's a tradeoff ,you cannot spend 3-4 hours day playing video games and say now I want to be more successful,it does not work that way,unless you are a gamer but you need to make sacrifices.The question is are you willing to make #sacrifices.
#young#success#leadership#business#career#entrepreneur#entrepreneurship

17.IRONMAN THEORY 5.

IRONMAN THEORIES..CHAPTER5...

IRONMAN RULE #####5" "SOMETIMES YOU HAVE TO RUN BEFORE YOU WALK" Conventional wisdom says,walk before you run.You always take that step by step process.You kinda climb the ladder,you have to do it in a very sequential manner but what I notice sometimes success is messy.Sometimes you don't necessarily do things sequentially.You might have to do things simultaneously.You are working on many things at the same time.You are putting out fire,you are solving problems.You are doing a lot of different things and sometimes to get what you want,you have to act as if there's no limit to your abilities.You have to act as if there's no ceiling,there's no restriction.There is no so much,oh once I know how to do that then I'll do it.Let me ask you a question, because most people what holds them back is I don't know do something,and when I hear that I always ask them-Does that mean you don't know how to do or you don't want to do it? Because you all have the ability to do it.Its just a question do you want it bad enough?You don't have to get it right: You have to get it going.

18.THE LIFE LESSON.

LIFE LESSON....

Take the responsibility for your actions at the time you perform your actions, not at the time you get caught. Which leads to a great leader ahead. #leadership#leadershipdevelopment#motivation#success.